Presented to

Virginia

From

Robin

On this date

Jan. 8 · 2022

Choose Joy

CREATIVE DEVOTIONAL

BARBOUR BOOKS
An Imprint of Barbour Publishing, Inc.

Readings are compiled and have been adapted from: *Daily Wisdom for Women 2013 Collection*; *Daily Wisdom for Women 2014 Collection*; *Everyday Joy, Everyday Encouragement, Everyday Hope*; and *365 Encouraging Verses of the Bible*. Published by Barbour Publishing, Inc. All rights reserved.

Scripture quotations marked NIV are taken from the HOLY BIBLE, NEW INTERNATIONAL VERSION®. NIV®. Copyright © 1973, 1978, 1984, 2011 by Biblica, Inc.™ Used by permission. All rights reserved worldwide.

Scripture quotations marked ESV are from The Holy Bible, English Standard Version®, copyright © 2001 by Crossway Bibles, a publishing ministry of Good News Publishers. Used by permission. All rights reserved.

Scripture quotations marked NLT are taken from the *Holy Bible*. New Living Translation copyright© 1996, 2004, 2015 by Tyndale House Foundation. Used by permission of Tyndale House Publishers, Inc. Carol Stream, Illinois 60188. All rights reserved.

Scripture quotations marked AMPC are taken from the Amplified® Bible, Classic Edition© 1954, 1958, 1962, 1964, 1965, 1987 by The Lockman Foundation. Used by permission.

Scripture quotations marked MSG are from *THE MESSAGE*. Copyright © by Eugene H. Peterson 1993, 1994, 1995, 1996, 2000, 2001, 2002. Used by permission of NavPress Publishing Group.

Scripture quotations marked KJV are taken from the King James Version of the Bible.

Scripture quotations marked NKJV are taken from the New King James Version®. Copyright © 1982 by Thomas Nelson, Inc. Used by permission. All rights reserved.

Published by Barbour Books, an imprint of Barbour Publishing, Inc., 1810 Barbour Drive, Uhrichsville, Ohio 44683, www.barbourbooks.com

Our mission is to inspire the world with the life-changing message of the Bible.

Member of the
Evangelical Christian
Publishers Association

Today. . .Choose Joy!

Experience the encouragement and delight that come your way each and every day that you *Choose Joy!* Featuring fifty-two powerful devotional readings complemented by creative coloring pages, this beautiful volume provides lovely insights and truth-filled biblical wisdom for your soul. Still your heart and mind as you reflect on these refreshing readings—and be drawn ever closer to the Joy-Giver Himself.

Sweet Aroma

The heartfelt counsel of a friend is as
sweet as perfume and incense.
PROVERBS 27:9 NLT

Whether it's over coffee, dessert, or even on the phone, a cherished friend can offer the encouragement and God-directed counsel we all need from time to time. Friendships that have Christ as their center are wonderful relationships blessed by the Father. Through the timely, godly advice these friends offer, God speaks to us, showering us with comfort that is as sweet as perfume and incense. So what are you waiting for? Make a date with a friend and share the sweet aroma of Jesus!

Jesus, Your friendship means the world to me. I value the close friendships You've blessed me with too! Thank You for the special women in my life. Show me every day how to be a blessing to them just as they are to me.

The BEST PLACE TO SEEK GOD is in a GARDEN.

GEORGE BERNARD SHAW

The New Me

*Therefore, if anyone is in Christ, the new creation
has come: The old has gone, the new is here!*
2 CORINTHIANS 5:17 NIV

Are you in Christ? Is He consistently Lord of your life? Then you are a new creation. *Everything* is new. What's history is done and over—and Jesus has replaced your old with His new: new peace, new joy, new love, new strength. Since God Himself sees us as a new creation, how can we do any less? We need to choose to see ourselves as a new creation too. And we can through God's grace. Be glad. Give thanks. Live each day as the new creation you have become through Jesus.

*Father, I'm so thankful that You are a God of grace—
and I thank You that I am a new creation. Please give
me the spiritual eyes to see myself as a new creation,
looking past the guilt of yesterday's choices.*

Release the Music Within

Those who are wise will find a time
and a way to do what is right.
ECCLESIASTES 8:5 NLT

It has been said that many people go to their graves with their music still in them. Do you carry a song within your heart, waiting to be heard?

Whether we are eight or eighty, it is never too late to surrender our hopes and dreams to God. A wise woman trusts that God will help her find the time and manner in which to use her talents for His glory as she seeks His direction. Let the music begin.

Dear Lord, my music is fading against the constant beat of a busy pace. I surrender my gifts to You and pray for the time and manner in which I can use those gifts to touch my world. Amen.

Sing, O YE HEAVENS, FOR the LORD HATH DONE IT: SHOUT, YE LOWER PARTS OF THE EARTH: BREAK FORTH INTO SINGING, ye mountains, O forest, AND EVERY TREE THEREIN.

ISAIAH 44:23

Simply Silly

A cheerful disposition is good for your health.
Proverbs 17:22 MSG

Imagine the effect we could have on our world today if our countenance reflected the joy of the Lord all of the time: at work, at home, at play. Jesus said, "I have told you this so that my joy may be in you and that your joy may be complete" (John 15:11 NIV). Is your cup of joy full? Have you laughed today? Not a small smile but laughter. Maybe it's time we looked for something to laugh about and tasted joy. Jesus suggested it.

Lord, help me find joy this day.
Let me laugh and give praises to the King. Amen.

Anxious Anticipations

I am not saying this because I am in need,
for I have learned to be content whatever the circumstances.

PHILIPPIANS 4:11 NIV

Have you ever been so eager for the future that you forgot to be thankful for the present day?

Humans tend to complain about the problems and irritations of life. It's much less natural to appreciate the good things we have—until they're gone. While it's fine to look forward to the future, let's remember to reflect on all of *today's* blessings—the large and the small—and appreciate all that we do have.

Thank You, Lord, for the beauty of today. Please remind me when I become preoccupied with the future and forget to enjoy the present.

EACH little FLOWER that OPENS

EACH LITTLE BIRD that SINGS

GOD MADE their GLOWING COLORS

AND MADE their TINY WINGS

CECIL FRANCES ALEXANDER

Refreshing Gift

For we have great joy and consolation in your love,
because the hearts of the saints have been
refreshed by you, brother.

PHILEMON 7 NKJV

Jesus always took the time for those who reached out to Him. In a crowd of people, He stopped to help a woman who touched Him. His quiet love extended to everyone who asked, whether verbally or with unspoken need. God brings people into our path who need our encouragement. We must consider those around us. Smile and thank the waitress, the cashier, the people who help in small ways. Cheering others can have the effect of an energizing drink of water so that they will be able to finish the race with a smile.

Jesus, thank You for being an example of how to encourage and refresh others. Help me to see their need and to be willing to reach out. Amen.

Infinite and Personal

Am I a God at hand,
saith the LORD, and not a God afar off?...
Do not I fill heaven and earth?
JEREMIAH 23:23-24 KJV

God says that He is both close at hand and over all there is. Whether your day is crumbling around you or is the best day you have ever had, do you see God in it? If the "sky is falling" or the sun is shining, do you still recognize the One who orders all the planets and all your days? Whether we see Him or not, God tells us He is there. And He's here too—in the good times and bad.

Lord, empower me to trust You when it's hard to remember that You are near. And help me to live thankfully when times are good. Amen.

Chosen

*Before I formed you in the womb I knew [and] approved of
you [as My chosen instrument], and before you were born
I separated and set you apart, consecrating you.*
JEREMIAH 1:5 AMPC

God said that before He formed Jeremiah in his mother's womb, He knew
him. God separated him from everyone else to perform a specific task,
and He consecrated him for that purpose. We can be sure that if God did
that for Jeremiah, He did it for each one of us. Nothing about us or our
circumstances surprises God. He knew about everything before we were
born. And He ordained that we should walk in those ways because we are
uniquely qualified by Him to do so. What an awesome God we serve!

*Father, the thought that You chose me before the foundation of the
world and set me apart for a specific calling is humbling. You are
so good. May I go forward with a renewed purpose in life.*

a bird
does not sing because
it has an answer.
It sings because
it has a
song.

CHINESE
PROVERB

God in the Details

"When we heard of it, our hearts melted in fear and everyone's courage failed because of you, for the LORD your God is God in heaven above and on the earth below."

JOSHUA 2:11 NIV

Sometimes, when our lives seem to be under siege from the demands of work, bills, family, whatever—finding the work of God amid the strife can be difficult. Even though we acknowledge His power, we may overlook the gentle touches, the small ways in which He makes every day a little easier. Just as the Lord cares for the tiniest bird (Matthew 10:29–31), so He seeks to be a part of every detail in your life. Look for Him there.

Father God, I know You are by my side every day, good or bad, and that You love and care for me. Help me to see Your work in my life and in the lives of my friends and family.

Practicality vs. Passion

Leaving her water jar, the woman went back to the town and said to the people, "Come, see a man who told me everything I ever did. Could this be the Messiah?"

JOHN 4:28–29 NIV

Practicality gave way to passion the day the woman at the well abandoned her task, lay down her jar, and ran into town. Everything changed the day she met a man at the well and He asked her for a drink of water. Although they had never met before, He told her everything she had ever done, and then He offered her living water that would never run dry. Do you live with such passion, or do you cling to your water jar? Has an encounter with Christ made an impact that cannot be denied in your life?

Lord, help me to lay down anything that stifles my passion for sharing the Good News with others. Amen.

Life Preservers

My comfort in my suffering is this:
Your promise preserves my life.
PSALM 119:50 NIV

In the difficulties of life, God is our life preserver. When we are battered by the waves of trouble, we can expect God to understand and to comfort us in our distress. His Word, like a buoyant life preserver, holds us up in the bad times. But the life preserver only works if you put it on *before* your boat sinks. God will surround you with His love and protection—even if you're unconscious of His presence. He promises to keep our heads above water in the storms of living.

Preserving God, I cling to You as my life preserver.
Keep my head above the turbulent water of caregiving
so I don't drown. Bring me safely to the shore.

A Shadow of the Past

"Only Rahab the prostitute and all who are with her in her house shall be spared, because she hid the spies we sent."

JOSHUA 6:17 NIV

Rahab wasn't trapped by her past. It didn't hold her back. She was used by God. Her name has come down to us centuries later because of her bold faith. We all have to deal with a past. But God is able to bring good from a painful past. By the grace and power of God, we can make choices in the present that can affect our future. There is transforming power with God. We have hope, no matter what lies behind us.

Holy Spirit, You are always at work. Don't ever stop! Show me a new way, Lord. Help me to make healthier choices for myself and my family. Thank You for Your renewing presence in my life.

Board God's Boat

Then, because so many people were coming and going that they did not even have a chance to eat, he said to them, "Come with me by yourselves to a quiet place and get some rest."

MARK 6:31 NIV

The apostles ministered tirelessly—so much so, they had little time to eat. The Lord noticed that they had neglected to take time for themselves. Sensitive to their needs, the Savior instructed them to retreat by boat with Him to a solitary place of rest where He was able to minister to them. Often, we allow the hectic pace of daily life to drain us physically and spiritually, and in the process, we deny ourselves time alone to pray and read God's Word. Meanwhile, God patiently waits. So perhaps it's time to board God's boat to a quieter place!

Heavenly Father, in my hectic life I've neglected time apart with You. Help me to board Your boat and stay afloat through spending time in Your Word and in prayer. Amen.

A Child in Need

"For all those things My hand has made, and all those things exist,"
says the LORD. "But on this one will I look: on him who is poor
and of a contrite spirit, and who trembles at My word."

ISAIAH 66:2 NKJV

A humble child of God with a need catches His eye. Though He is always watching over all of us, He is drawn to a child who needs Him. We may need forgiveness, wisdom, courage, endurance, patience, health, protection, or even love. God promises to come to our aid when He sees us with a hand up, reaching for His assistance. What needs do you have in your life today? Raise your hand in prayer to God. He'll take care of your needs and then some—blessing your life in ways you can't even imagine!

Father, thank You for caring about the needs of Your children.
Help me to remember to always seek You first.

The Secret of Serendipity

A happy heart makes the face cheerful.
PROVERBS 15:13 NIV

Can you remember the last time you laughed in wild abandon? Better yet, when was the last time you did something fun, outrageous, or out of the ordinary? Perhaps it is an activity you haven't done since you were a child, like slip down a waterslide, strap on a pair of ice skates, or pitch a tent and camp overnight. A happy heart turns life's situations into opportunities for fun. When we seek innocent pleasures, we glean the benefits of a happy heart. So try a bit of whimsy just for fun, and rediscover the secret of serendipity.

Dear Lord, because of You, I have a happy heart.
Lead me to do something fun and spontaneous today! Amen.

A Very Important Phrase

And it came to pass. . .
Found More Than 400 Times in the King James Bible

There are times in life when we think we can't bear one more day, one more hour, one more minute. But no matter how bad things seem at the time, they are temporary. What's really important is how we handle the opportunities before us today, whether we let our trials defeat us or look for the hand of God in everything. Every day, week, and year are made up of things that "come to pass"—so even if we fail, we needn't be disheartened. Other opportunities—better days—will come. Let's look past those hard things today and glorify the name of the Lord.

Lord Jesus, how awesome it is that You send or allow these little things that will pass. May we recognize Your hand in them today and praise You for them.

The White Knight

*Then I will rejoice in the L*ORD*.*
I will be glad because he rescues me.
PSALM 35:9 NLT

We're all waiting for someone to rescue us. We wait and wait and wait. . . .
The truth is, God doesn't want you to exist in a perpetual state of waiting.
Live your life—your whole life—by seeking daily joy in the Savior of your
soul, Jesus Christ. And here's the best news of all: He's already done the
rescuing by dying on the cross for our sins! He's the *true* white knight
who secured your eternity in heaven. Stop waiting; seek His face today!

Jesus, I praise You because You are the rescuer of my soul.
Remind me of this fact when I'm looking for relief in other
people and places. You take care of my present and
eternal needs, and for that I am grateful. Amen.

Is Anyone Listening?

And I will ask the Father, and He will give you another Comforter
(Counselor, Helper, Intercessor, Advocate, Strengthener,
and Standby), that He may remain with you forever.
JOHN 14:16 AMPC

Our heavenly Father wants to hear from us. He cares so much that He sent the Holy Spirit to be our Counselor, our Comforter. When we pray—when we tell God our needs and give Him praise—He listens. Then He directs the Spirit within us to speak to our hearts and give us reassurance. Our world is filled with noise and distractions. Look for a place where you can be undisturbed for a few minutes. Take a deep breath, lift your prayers, and listen. God will speak—and your heart will hear.

Dear Lord, I thank You for Your care.
Help me to recognize Your voice and to listen well.

A Comfortable Place

Don't you realize that your body is the temple of the
Holy Spirit, who lives in you and was given to
you by God? You do not belong to yourself.

1 CORINTHIANS 6:19 NLT

We take the time to make our homes comfortable and beautiful when we know visitors are coming. In the same way, we ought to prepare our hearts for the Holy Spirit who lives inside of us. We should daily ask God to help us clean up the junk in our hearts. We should take special care to tune up our bodies through exercise, eating healthful foods, and dressing attractively and modestly. Our bodies belong to God. Taking care of ourselves shows others that we honor God enough to respect and use wisely what He has given us.

Dear Lord, thank You for letting me belong to You.
May my body be a comfortable place for You. Amen.

Who Helps the Helper?

The Lord is my strength and my shield; my heart trusted in him,
and I am helped: therefore my heart greatly rejoiceth;
and with my song will I praise him.
PSALM 28:7 KJV

Helping can be exhausting. The needs of young children, teens, grandchildren, aging parents, our neighbors, and fellow church members—the list is never-ending—can stretch us until we're ready to snap. And then we find that *we* need help. Who helps the helper? The Lord does. When we are weak, He is strong. When we are vulnerable, He is our shield. When we can no longer trust in our own resources, we can trust in Him. He is always there, ready to help. Rejoice in Him, praise His name, and you will find the strength to go on.

Father, I'm worn out. I can't care for all the people and needs
You bring into my life by myself. I need Your strength.
Thank You for being my helper and my shield.

Magnifying Life

My soul makes its boast in the Lord; let the humble hear and be glad.
Oh, magnify the Lord with me, and let us exalt his name together!
PSALM 34:2-3 ESV

Mary knew she was the object of God's favor and mercy. That knowledge produced humility. Try as we might, we can't produce this humility in ourselves. It is our natural tendency to be self-promoters. . .to better our own reputations. We need the help of the Spirit to remind us that God has favored each of us with His presence. He did not have to come to us in Christ, but He did. He has chosen to set His love on us. His life redeemed ours, and He sanctifies us. We are recipients of the action of His grace.

Christ Jesus, help me to remember what You have done
for me and desire for others to see and know You.

No More Sting

O death, where is thy sting? O grave, where is thy victory?
1 Corinthians 15:55 KJV

We have a choice to make. We can either live life in fear or live life by faith. Fear and faith cannot coexist. Jesus Christ has conquered our greatest fear—death. He rose victorious and has given us eternal life through faith. Knowing this truth enables us to courageously face our fears. There is no fear that cannot be conquered by faith. Let's not panic but trust the Lord instead. Let's live by faith and experience the victory that has been given to us through Jesus Christ, our Lord.

Lord, You alone know my fears. Help me to trust You more.
May I walk in the victory that You have purchased for me. Amen.

Well-Watered

"The Lord will guide you always; he will satisfy your needs in a sun-scorched land and will strengthen your frame. You will be like a well-watered garden, like a spring whose waters never fail."

ISAIAH 58:11 NIV

We need a downpour of God's Word and the Holy Spirit's presence in our parched spirits. Not an occasional sprinkle, but a soul soaking to replenish our frazzled bodies and weary minds. We know this soaking comes from consistent Bible study, the necessary pruning of confessed sin, and prayer time. These produce a well-watered garden, fruitful and lush, mirroring God's beauty, creating a life to which others are drawn to come and linger in His refreshing presence.

Eternal Father, strengthen my frame, guide my paths, and satisfy my needs as only You can. Make my life a well-watered garden, fruitful for You and Your purposes. Amen.

GOD is writing A STORY of FAITH through your LIFE.

A Better Offer

"So in everything, do to others what
you would have them do to you."
MATTHEW 7:12 NIV

Jesus took responsibilities, commitments, and obligations seriously. In fact, Jesus said, "All you need to say is simply 'Yes' or 'No'; anything beyond this comes from the evil one" (Matthew 5:37 NIV). Satan desires for us to be stressed out, overcommitted, and not able to do anything well. Satan delights when we treat others in an unkind, offensive manner. However, God, upon request, will help us prioritize our commitments so that our "yes" is "yes" and our "no" is "no." Then in everything we do, we are liberated to do to others as we would have them do to us.

Lord, please prioritize my commitments to enable me in everything
to do to others as I would desire for them to do to me. Amen.

Put on a Happy Face

*He restoreth my soul: he leadeth me in the paths
of righteousness for his name's sake.*

PSALM 23:3 KJV

Our God is not a God of negativity but of possibility. He will guide us through our difficulties and beyond them. Today we should turn our thoughts and prayers toward Him. Focus on a hymn or a praise song and play it in your mind. Praise chases away the doldrums and tips our lips up in a smile. With a renewed spirit of optimism and hope, we can thank the Giver of all things good. Thankfulness to the Father can turn our plastic smiles into real ones, and as the psalm states, our souls will be restored.

*Father, I'm down in the dumps today. You are my unending source
of strength. Gather me in Your arms for always. Amen.*

One Step at a Time

With your help I can advance against a troop;
with my God I can scale a wall.
PSALM 18:29 NIV

We often become discouraged when we face a mountain-size task. Whether it's weight loss or a graduate degree or our income taxes, some things just seem impossible. And they often *can't* be done—not all at once. Tasks like these are best faced one step at a time. One pound at a time. Chipping away instead of moving the whole mountain at once. With patience, perseverance, and God's help, your goals may be more attainable than you think.

Dear Father, the task before me seems impossible.
However, I know I can do it with Your help. I pray
that I will trust You every step of the way. Amen.

Mirror Image

Behold, thou art fair, my love; behold,
thou art fair; thou hast doves' eyes.
SONG OF SOLOMON 1:15 KJV

No matter how hard we try, when the focus is on self, we see shortcomings. Our only hope is to see ourselves through a different mirror. We must remember that as we grow as Christians, we take on the characteristics of Christ. The more we become like Him, the more beautiful we are in our own eyes and to those around us. God loves to behold us when we are covered in Christ. The mirror image He sees has none of the blemishes or imperfections, only the beauty.

Oh God, thank You for beholding me as being fair and valuable.
Help me to see myself through Your eyes. Amen.

Rejoicing with Friends

*"Then he calls his friends and neighbors together and says,
'Rejoice with me; I have found my lost sheep.'"*
LUKE 15:6 NIV

Think of all the reasons you have to celebrate. Are you in good health? Have you overcome a tough obstacle? Are you handling your finances without much grief? Doing well at your job? Bonding with friends or family? If so, then throw yourself a party and invite a friend. Better yet, call your friends and neighbors together, as the scripture indicates. Share your praises with people who will truly appreciate all that the Lord is doing in your life. Let the party begin!

Lord, thank You that I'm created in the image of a God who knows how to celebrate. I have so many reasons to rejoice today. Thank You for Your many blessings. And today I especially want to thank You for giving me friends to share my joys and sorrows.

Why Me?

I am Alpha and Omega, the beginning and the ending, saith the Lord,
which is, and which was, and which is to come, the Almighty.

REVELATION 1:8 KJV

When God spoke our world into existence, He called into being a certain reality, knowing then everything that ever was to happen—and everyone who ever was to be. That you exist now is cause for rejoicing! God made *you* to fellowship with Him! If that fellowship demands trials for a season, rejoice that God thinks you worthy to share in the sufferings of Christ—and, eventually, in His glory. Praise His holy name!

Father, I thank You for giving me this difficult time in my life.
Shine through all my trials today. I want You to get the glory.

Faith, the Emotional Balancer

No man is justified by the law in the sight of God,
it is evident: for, The just shall live by faith.
GALATIANS 3:11 KJV

Emotions mislead us. One day shines with promise as we bounce out of bed in song, while the next day dims in despair and we'd prefer to hide under the bedcovers. It has been said that faith is the bird that feels the light and sings to greet the dawn while it is still dark. The Bible instructs us to live by faith—not by feelings. Faith assures us that daylight will dawn in our darkest moments, affirming God's presence so that even when we fail to pray and positive feelings fade, our moods surrender to song.

Heavenly Father, I desire for my faith, not my emotions, to dictate
my life. I pray for balance in my hide-under-the-cover days,
so that I might surrender to You in song. Amen.

Choose Life

*"The thief comes only to steal and kill and destroy;
I have come that they may have life, and have it to the full."*
JOHN 10:10 NIV

God's Word shows us the lie—and the "liar"—behind defeating thoughts. We have an enemy who delights in our believing negative things, an enemy who wants only destruction for our souls. But Jesus came to give us life! We only have to choose it as an act of the will blended with faith. When we rely on Him alone, He'll enable us to not only survive but *thrive* in our daily routine. Each day let's make a conscious decision to take hold of what Christ offers us—life to the full.

*Loving Lord, help me daily to choose You and the life You
want to give me. Give me the eyes of faith to trust
that You will enable me to serve lovingly.*

Annual or Perennial?

They are like trees planted along the riverbank, bearing fruit each season. Their leaves never wither, and they prosper in all they do.
Psalm 1:3 nlt

Annuals or perennials? Each has its advantages. Annuals are inexpensive, provide instant gratification, and keep boredom from setting in. Perennials require an initial investment, but when properly tended, faithfully provide beauty year after year—long after the annuals have dried up and withered away. Perennials are designed for the long haul—not just short-term enjoyment but long-term beauty. The application to our lives is twofold. First, be a perennial—long-lasting, enduring, slow-growing, steady, and faithful. Second, don't be discouraged by your inevitable dormant seasons. Tend to your soul, and it will reward you with years of lush blossoms.

Father, be the gardener of my soul. Amen.

Have You Looked Up?

The heavens proclaim the glory of God. The skies display his craftsmanship. Day after day they continue to speak; night after night they make him known.

PSALM 19:1-2 NLT

God has placed glimpses of creation's majesty—evidence of His love—throughout our world. Sunsets, seashells, flowers, snowflakes, changing seasons, moonlit shadows. Such glories are right in front of us every single day! But we must develop eyes to see these reminders in our daily life and not let the cares and busyness of our lives keep our heads turned down. Have you looked up today?

Lord, open my eyes! Unstuff my ears! Teach me to see the wonders of Your creation every day and to point them out to my children.

Faultless

To him who is able to keep you from stumbling and to present you before his glorious presence without fault and with great joy.

JUDE 24 NIV

Jesus loves us so much despite our shortcomings. He is the One who can keep us from falling—who can present us faultless before the Father. Because of this, we can have our joy restored no matter what. Whether we have done wrong and denied it or have been falsely accused, we can come into His presence to be restored and lifted up. Let us keep our eyes on Him instead of on our need to justify ourselves to God or others.

Thank You, Jesus, for Your cleansing love and for the joy we can find in Your presence. Amen.

Reflecting God in Our Work

Whatever you do, work at it with all your heart,
as working for the Lord, not for human masters.

COLOSSIANS 3:23 NIV

As believers, we are God's children. No one is perfect, and for this there is grace. However, we may be the only reflection of our heavenly Father that some will ever see. Our attitudes and actions on the job speak volumes to those around us. Although it may be tempting to do just enough to get by, we put forth our best effort when we remember we represent God to the world. A Christian's character on the job should be a positive reflection of the Lord.

Father, help me today to represent You well through my work.
I want to reflect Your love in all I do. Amen.

AND HE has promised US LIFE THAT LASTS FOREVER!

1 JOHN 2:25

Just Half a Cup

"I am coming to you now, but I say these things while I am still in the world, so that they may have the full measure of my joy within them."

JOHN 17:13 NIV

Our heavenly Father longs to bestow His richest blessings and wisdom on us. He loves us, so He desires to fill our cup to overflowing with the things that He knows will bring us pleasure and growth. Do you tell Him to stop pouring when your cup is only half full? You may not even realize it, but perhaps your actions dictate that your cup remains half empty. Seek a full cup and enjoy the full measure of the joy of the Lord.

Dear Jesus, forgive me for not accepting the fullness of Your blessings and Your joy. Help me to see the ways that I prevent my cup from being filled to overflowing. Thank You for wanting me to have the fullness of Your joy. Amen.

Hide and Seek

"And do you seek great things for yourself? Seek them not, for behold,
I am bringing disaster upon all flesh, declares the LORD."
JEREMIAH 45:5 ESV

God warns us: *Don't seek great things.* The more we seek them, the more elusive they become. As soon as we think we have them in our grasp, they disappear. If we commit to more activities than we can realistically handle, the best result is that we can't follow through. Worse, we might make them our god. Jesus tells us what we should seek: the kingdom of God and His righteousness (Matthew 6:33). When we seek the right things, He'll give us every good and perfect gift (James 1:17). And that will be more than we can ask or dream.

Lord, please teach me to seek not greatness but You.
May You be the all in all of my life.

Location, Location, Location

Those who live in the shelter of the Most High will find rest in the shadow of the Almighty. This I declare about the LORD: He alone is my refuge, my place of safety; he is my God, and I trust him.

PSALM 91:1-2 NLT

If something is getting you down in life, check your location. Where are your thoughts? Let what the world has conditioned you to think go in one ear and out the other. Stand on the truth, the promises of God's Word. Say of the Lord, "God is my refuge! I am hidden in Christ! Nothing can harm me. In Him I trust!" Say it loud. Say it often. Say it over and over until it becomes your reality. And you will find yourself dwelling in that secret place every moment of the day.

God, You are my refuge. When I abide in You, nothing can harm me. Your Word is the truth on which I rely. Fill me with Your light and the peace of Your love. It's You and me, Lord, all the way! Amen.

Light My Path

Your word is a lamp for my feet,
a light on my path.
PSALM 119:105 NIV

God's Word is like a streetlamp. Often, we *think* we know where we're going and where the stumbling blocks are. We believe we can avoid pitfalls and maneuver the path successfully on our own. But the truth is that without God's Word, we are walking in darkness, stumbling and tripping. When we sincerely begin to search God's Word, we find the path becomes clear. God's light allows us to live our lives in the most fulfilling way possible, a way planned out from the very beginning by God Himself.

Jesus, shine Your light upon my path. I have spent too long wandering
through the darkness, looking for my way. As I search Your Word,
I ask You to make it a lamp to my feet so that I can avoid
the pitfalls of the world and walk safely along the
path You have created specifically for me.

Power Up

The Spirit of God, who raised Jesus from the dead, lives in you.
ROMANS 8:11 NLT

God is the same yesterday, today, and forever. His strength does not diminish over time. That same mountain-moving power you read about in the lives of people from the Old and New Testaments still exists today. We don't have to go it alone. Our heavenly Father wants to help. All we have to do is ask. He has already made His power available to His children. Whatever we face—wherever we go—whatever dreams we have for our lives, take courage and know that anything is possible when we draw on the power of God.

*Father, help me to remember that You are always with me,
ready to help me do all things. Amen.*

Comfort Food

For whatever things were written before were written for our learning, that we through the patience and comfort of the Scriptures might have hope.

ROMANS 15:4 NKJV

Romans 15:4 tells us that the scriptures are comfort food for the soul. They were written and given so that, through our learning, we would be comforted with the truths of God. Worldly pleasures bring a temporary comfort, but the problem still remains when the pleasure or comfort fades. However, the words of God are soothing and provide permanent hope and peace. Through God's Word, you will be changed, and your troubles will dim in the bright light of Christ. So the next time you are sad, lonely, or disappointed, turn to the Word of God as your source of comfort.

Thank You, Father, for the rich comfort Your Word provides. Help me to remember to find my comfort in scripture rather than through earthly things that will ultimately fail me. Amen.

Can God Interrupt You?

*In their hearts humans plan their course,
but the LORD establishes their steps.*
PROVERBS 16:9 NIV

Have you ever considered that perhaps God has ordained our interruptions? Perhaps, just perhaps, God may be trying to get your attention. There is nothing wrong with planning our day. However, we have such limited vision. God sees the big picture. Be open. Be flexible. Allow God to change your plans in order to accomplish His divine purposes. Instead of becoming frustrated, look for ways the Lord might be working. Be willing to join Him. When we do, interruptions become blessings.

*Dear Lord, forgive me when I am so rigidly locked into my own
agenda that I miss Yours. Give me Your eternal perspective
so that I may be open to divine interruptions. Amen.*

Marvelous Thunder

"God's voice thunders in marvelous ways;
he does great things beyond our understanding."
JOB 37:5 NIV

Have you ever reflected deeply on the power that God is? Not that He *has*, but that He is.

Consider this: The One who controls nature also holds every one of our tears in His hand. He is our Father, and He works on our behalf. He is more than enough to meet our needs; He does things far beyond what our human minds can understand. This One who is power loves you. He looks at you and says, "I delight in you, My daughter." Wow! His ways are marvelous and beyond understanding.

Lord God, You are power. You hold all things in Your hand
and You chose to love me. You see my actions, hear my
thoughts, watch my heartbreak. . .and You still love me.
Please help me trust in Your power, never my own.

blessings *brighten* WHEN *we count them.*

(MALTBIE D. BABCOCK)

Eye Care

For thus says the LORD of hosts. . .
"he who touches you touches the apple of His eye."
ZECHARIAH 2:8 NKJV

To think that we are the apple of God's eye is incredible. Consider the care He must take for us. He will go to great lengths to protect us from harm. When something or someone does attack us, God feels our pain. He is instantly aware of our discomfort for it is His own. When the storms of life come, we must remember how God feels each twinge of suffering. Despite the adversity, we can praise God for He is sheltering us.

Thank You, God, that You are so aware of what is happening
to me. Thank You for Your protection. Amen.

God's Mountain Sanctuary

And seeing the multitudes, he went up into a mountain:
and. . .his disciples came unto him: And he
opened his mouth and taught them.
MATTHEW 5:1-2 KJV

Jesus often retreated to a mountain to pray. There He called His disciples to depart from the multitudes so that He could teach them valuable truths—the lessons we learn from nature. Do you yearn for a place where problems evaporate like the morning dew? Do you need a place of solace? God is wherever you are—behind a bedroom door, nestled alongside you in your favorite chair, or even standing at a sink full of dirty dishes. Come apart and enter God's mountain sanctuary.

Heavenly Father, I long to hear Your voice and to flow
in the path You clear before me. Help me to find
sanctuary in Your abiding presence. Amen.

A Fragrant Offering

*Follow God's example, therefore, as dearly loved children and walk
in the way of love, just as Christ loved us and gave himself
up for us as a fragrant offering and sacrifice to God.*

EPHESIANS 5:1-2 NIV

If we carry the scent of Christ in our daily walk, people will be drawn to us and want to "stay for a while." But how do we give off that amazing, inviting fragrance? There's really only one way—by imitating God. By loving others fully. By seeing them through His eyes. By looking with great compassion on those who are hurting, as Jesus did when He went about healing the sick and pouring out His life for those in need. As we live a life of love in front of those we care for, we exude the sweetest fragrance of all—Christ.

*Dear Lord, I long to live a life that points people to You. As I care
for those in need, may the sweet-smelling aroma of You and
Your love be an invitation for people to draw near.*

Ladies in Waiting

*I will wait for the L*ORD*. . . . I will put my trust in him.*
ISAIAH 8:17 NIV

Do we want joy without accepting heartache? Peace without living through the stress? Patience without facing demands? God sees things differently. He's giving us the opportunity to learn through these delays, irritations, and struggles. Like Isaiah, we need to learn the art of waiting on God. He will come through every time—but in *His* time not ours. The wait may be hours or days, or it could be years. But God is always faithful to provide for us. It is when we learn to wait on Him that we will find joy, peace, and patience through the struggle.

Father, You know what I need, so I will wait. Help me be patient, knowing that You control my situation and that all good things come in Your time.

When I Think of the Heavens

When I consider your heavens, the work of your fingers, the moon
and the stars, which you have set in place, what is mankind that
you are mindful of them, human beings that you care for them?
PSALM 8:3-4 NIV

Daughter of God, you are important to your heavenly Father, more important
than the sun, the moon, and the stars. You are created in the image of God,
and He cares for you. In fact, He cares so much that He sent His Son, Jesus,
to offer His life as a sacrifice for your sins. The next time you look up at the
heavens, the next time you *ooh* and *aah* over a majestic mountain or emerald
waves crashing against the shoreline, remember that those things, in all
of their splendor, don't even come close to you—God's greatest creation.

Oh Father, when I look at everything You have created, I'm so
overwhelmed with who You are. Who am I that You would
think twice about me? And yet You do. You love me,
and for that I'm eternally grateful!

The Dream-Maker

*"No eye has seen, no ear has heard, and no mind has imagined
what God has prepared for those who love him."*

1 CORINTHIANS 2:9 NLT

Dreams, goals, and expectations are part of our daily lives. We have an idea of what we want and how we're going to achieve it. Disappointment can raise its ugly head when what we wanted—what we expected—doesn't happen like we thought it should or doesn't happen as fast as we planned. God knows the dreams He has placed inside of you. He created you and knows what you can do even better than you know yourself. Maintain your focus—not on the dream but on the Dream Maker—and together you will achieve your dream.

*God, thank You for putting dreams in my heart. I refuse to quit.
I'm looking to You to show me how to reach my dreams. Amen.*

A Heavenly Party

"I tell you that in the same way there will be more rejoicing in heaven over one sinner who repents than over ninety-nine righteous persons who do not need to repent."
LUKE 15:7 NIV

The Father threw your very own party on the moment you accepted His Son as your Savior. Did you experience a taste of that party from the response of your spiritual mentors here on earth? As Christians, we should celebrate with our new brothers and sisters in Christ every chance we get. If you haven't yet taken that step in your faith, don't wait! Heaven's party planners are eager to get your celebration started.

Father, I am so grateful that You rejoice in new Christians. Strengthen my desire to reach the lost while I am here on earth. Then, when I reach heaven, the heavenly parties will be all the sweeter! Amen.

Anxiety Check!

Do not be anxious about anything, but in every situation,
by prayer and petition, with thanksgiving, present your requests to God.
PHILIPPIANS 4:6 NIV

Checking to make sure we've locked the door, turned off the stove, and unplugged the curling iron just comes naturally. So why do we forget some of the bigger checks in life? Take anxiety, for instance. When was the last time you did an anxiety check? Days? Weeks? Months? Chances are, you're due for another. After all, we're instructed not to be anxious about anything. Instead, we're to present our requests to God with thanksgiving in our hearts. We're to turn to Him in prayer so that He can take our burdens. Once they've lifted, it's bye-bye anxiety!

Father, I get anxious sometimes. And I don't always remember
to turn to You with my anxiety. In fact, I forget to check
for anxiety at all. Today I hand my anxieties to You.
Thank You that I can present my requests to You.

A Strong Heart

Whom have I in heaven but you? And earth has nothing I desire besides you. My flesh and my heart may fail, but God is the strength of my heart and my portion forever.

PSALM 73:25–26 NIV

You don't have to be strong. In your weakness, God's strength shines through. And His strength surpasses anything you could produce, even on your best day. It's the same strength that spoke the heavens and the earth into existence. The same strength that parted the Red Sea. And it's the same strength that made the journey up the hill to the cross. So how do you tap into that strength? There's really only one way. Come into His presence. Spend some quiet time with Him. Allow His strong arms to encompass you. God is all you will ever need.

Father, I feel so weak at times. It's hard just to put one foot in front of the other. But I know You are my strength. Invigorate me with that strength today, Lord.

Going Above and Beyond

Now to him who is able to do immeasurably more than all we ask
or imagine, according to his power that is at work within us,
to him be glory in the church and in Christ Jesus
throughout all generations, for ever and ever!
EPHESIANS 3:20–21 NIV

Think for a moment. . . . What have you asked for? What have you imagined? It's amazing to think that God, in His infinite power and wisdom, can do immeasurably more than all that! How? According to the power that is at work within us. It's not our power, thankfully. We don't have enough power to scrape the surface of what we'd like to see done in our lives. But His power in us gets the job done. . .and more. Praise the Lord! Praise Him in the church and throughout all generations! He's an immeasurable God.

Heavenly Father, I feel pretty powerless at times. It's amazing to realize
You have more power in Your little finger than all of mankind has
put together. Today I praise You for being a God who goes
above and beyond all I could ask or imagine.

More Inspiration for Your Creative Soul

Choose Joy: 3-Minute Devotions for Women
978-1-63409-998-1

Choose Prayer: 3-Minute Devotions for Women
978-1-68322-398-6

Choose Grace: 3-Minute Devotions for Women
978-1-68322-255-2

Choose Hope: 3-Minute Devotions for Women
978-1-68322-174-6

Got 3 minutes to spare? You'll find the spiritual pick-me-up you crave in these inspiring 3-minute devotionals. Written especially the twenty-first-century woman, these delightful books pack a powerful dose of comfort, encouragement, and hope into just-right-sized readings. Minute 1: scripture to meditate on; Minute 2: a short devotional reading; Minute 3: a prayer to jump-start a conversation with God.

Paperback / $4.99 each